50 Premium Sandwich Dinner Recipes

By: Kelly Johnson

Table of Contents

- Classic French Dip
- Steak and Cheese Hoagie
- Grilled Cheese with Tomato Soup
- Lobster Roll
- Pulled Pork with Coleslaw Sandwich
- Chicken Parmesan Sandwich
- Turkey and Cranberry Brie Sandwich
- Philly Cheesesteak
- Roast Beef and Horseradish Sandwich
- Portobello Mushroom and Goat Cheese Sandwich
- Shrimp Po' Boy
- Grilled Chicken Club Sandwich
- Smoked Salmon and Cream Cheese Bagel
- Veggie and Hummus Wrap
- Grilled Chicken and Avocado Sandwich
- Croque Monsieur
- BBQ Chicken Sliders
- Chicken Caesar Wrap
- Reuben Sandwich
- Chicken and Waffle Sandwich
- Caprese Sandwich
- Bacon, Egg, and Cheese Biscuit
- Tuna Salad Sandwich
- BLT with Avocado
- Meatball Sub
- Chicken and Pesto Panini
- Philly Chicken Cheesesteak
- Egg Salad Sandwich with Pickles
- Grilled Veggie and Mozzarella Sandwich
- Smoked Brisket Sandwich
- Fried Green Tomato BLT
- Crab Cake Sandwich with Remoulade
- Grilled Cheese with Apple and Bacon
- Mahi Mahi Fish Tacos
- Grilled Tuna Melt

- Spicy Sausage and Peppers Sandwich
- Pulled BBQ Jackfruit Sandwich
- Italian Sub Sandwich
- Buffalo Chicken Wrap
- Roast Beef and Swiss Sandwich
- Breakfast Burrito Sandwich
- Falafel Pita with Tzatziki
- Philly Steak and Egg Sandwich
- Cuban Sandwich
- Veggie and Quinoa Wrap
- Grilled Shrimp and Avocado Sandwich
- Lobster and Bacon Club Sandwich
- Spicy Chicken Banh Mi
- Grilled Salmon and Cucumber Sandwich
- Pulled Chicken and Mango Slaw Sandwich

Classic French Dip

Ingredients:

- 1 lb roast beef, thinly sliced
- 4 hoagie rolls
- 1 cup beef broth
- 1 tablespoon Worcestershire sauce
- 1 tablespoon soy sauce
- 1 clove garlic, minced
- 1/2 onion, thinly sliced
- 4 slices Swiss cheese
- Salt and freshly ground black pepper

Instructions:

1. Preheat the oven to 350°F (175°C). Slice the hoagie rolls and place them on a baking sheet.
2. In a saucepan, combine beef broth, Worcestershire sauce, soy sauce, and minced garlic. Heat over medium until warmed.
3. In a skillet, sauté the onions until soft, about 5 minutes. Add the sliced roast beef to warm through.
4. Assemble the sandwiches by layering the beef and onions on the rolls. Top with Swiss cheese and bake for 5-7 minutes until the cheese melts.
5. Serve with warm beef broth for dipping.

Steak and Cheese Hoagie

Ingredients:

- 1 lb ribeye steak, thinly sliced
- 4 hoagie rolls
- 1 onion, thinly sliced
- 1 bell pepper, sliced
- 1/2 cup provolone cheese, sliced
- 2 tablespoons olive oil
- Salt and freshly ground black pepper

Instructions:

1. Heat the olive oil in a skillet over medium-high heat. Add the onions and bell peppers, sautéing until softened, about 5 minutes.
2. Add the sliced steak to the pan, cooking until browned and cooked through, about 4-5 minutes.
3. Slice the hoagie rolls and fill with the steak, onions, and peppers. Top with provolone cheese and broil in the oven for 2-3 minutes until the cheese is melted.

Grilled Cheese with Tomato Soup

Ingredients:

- 4 slices bread
- 4 slices cheddar cheese
- 2 tablespoons butter
- 1 can (14 oz) tomato soup
- 1/2 teaspoon garlic powder
- 1/4 teaspoon dried basil

Instructions:

1. Heat a pan over medium heat. Butter one side of each slice of bread. Place one slice of cheese between two slices of bread and grill until golden brown on both sides.
2. In a saucepan, heat the tomato soup, garlic powder, and dried basil until warm.
3. Serve the grilled cheese sandwiches with a side of tomato soup for dipping.

Lobster Roll

Ingredients:

- 2 lobster tails, cooked and chopped
- 1/4 cup mayonnaise
- 1 tablespoon fresh lemon juice
- 1 tablespoon chopped fresh parsley
- 2 New England-style hot dog buns
- 1 tablespoon butter

Instructions:

1. In a bowl, combine the lobster, mayonnaise, lemon juice, and parsley. Season with salt and pepper to taste.
2. Butter the buns and toast them in a skillet until golden brown.
3. Fill the buns with the lobster mixture and serve immediately.

Pulled Pork with Coleslaw Sandwich

Ingredients:

- 2 cups pulled pork (cooked and shredded)
- 1/2 cup barbecue sauce
- 2 cups coleslaw
- 4 soft sandwich rolls

Instructions:

1. Heat the pulled pork in a skillet and mix with barbecue sauce.
2. Assemble the sandwiches by placing the pulled pork on the rolls, followed by a generous scoop of coleslaw.
3. Serve with pickles and extra barbecue sauce if desired.

Chicken Parmesan Sandwich

Ingredients:

- 2 chicken breasts, breaded and fried
- 1/2 cup marinara sauce
- 4 slices mozzarella cheese
- 4 sandwich rolls
- Fresh basil leaves (optional)

Instructions:

1. Heat the marinara sauce and cook the breaded chicken breasts until golden brown.
2. Top each chicken breast with marinara sauce and mozzarella cheese. Broil for 2-3 minutes until the cheese is melted.
3. Assemble the sandwiches on the rolls and garnish with fresh basil leaves, if desired.

Turkey and Cranberry Brie Sandwich

Ingredients:

- 4 slices turkey breast
- 2 tablespoons cranberry sauce
- 4 slices brie cheese
- 4 slices sourdough bread
- Butter for grilling

Instructions:

1. Butter one side of each slice of sourdough bread.
2. Layer the turkey, cranberry sauce, and brie cheese between two slices of bread.
3. Grill the sandwich on medium heat until golden brown on both sides and the cheese is melted.

Philly Cheesesteak

Ingredients:

- 1 lb ribeye steak, thinly sliced
- 4 hoagie rolls
- 1 onion, sliced
- 1 bell pepper, sliced
- 4 slices provolone cheese
- 2 tablespoons olive oil
- Salt and freshly ground black pepper

Instructions:

1. Heat olive oil in a skillet over medium-high heat. Sauté the onions and bell peppers until softened, about 5 minutes.
2. Add the steak to the pan and cook until browned and cooked through, about 4-5 minutes.
3. Toast the hoagie rolls and fill with the steak mixture. Top with provolone cheese and broil for 1-2 minutes until melted.

Roast Beef and Horseradish Sandwich

Ingredients:

- 2 cups thinly sliced roast beef
- 4 sandwich rolls
- 1/4 cup horseradish sauce
- 1 tablespoon Dijon mustard
- Fresh arugula or lettuce

Instructions:

1. Mix the horseradish sauce and Dijon mustard together.
2. Assemble the sandwiches by spreading the horseradish sauce mixture on the rolls. Add the roast beef and top with fresh arugula or lettuce.

Portobello Mushroom and Goat Cheese Sandwich

Ingredients:

- 2 large portobello mushrooms, cleaned and stems removed
- 2 tablespoons olive oil
- 1/4 cup goat cheese
- 2 sandwich rolls
- 1 tablespoon balsamic vinegar
- Fresh basil leaves

Instructions:

1. Heat olive oil in a skillet over medium heat. Sauté the mushrooms until tender, about 5 minutes per side.
2. Drizzle with balsamic vinegar and cook for an additional minute.
3. Assemble the sandwiches by placing the mushrooms on the rolls, adding goat cheese and fresh basil leaves.

Shrimp Po' Boy

Ingredients:

- 1 lb shrimp, peeled and deveined
- 1 cup flour
- 1/2 teaspoon paprika
- 1/2 teaspoon garlic powder
- Salt and freshly ground black pepper
- 4 sandwich rolls
- 1/2 cup lettuce, shredded
- 1/4 cup tomatoes, sliced
- 1/4 cup pickles, sliced
- 1/2 cup remoulade sauce (or tartar sauce)

Instructions:

1. Mix the flour, paprika, garlic powder, salt, and pepper in a bowl. Dredge the shrimp in the flour mixture.
2. Heat oil in a skillet over medium-high heat. Fry the shrimp until golden and cooked through, about 2-3 minutes per side.
3. Toast the sandwich rolls. Assemble the Po' Boy by placing shrimp on the rolls and topping with lettuce, tomatoes, pickles, and remoulade sauce.

Grilled Chicken Club Sandwich

Ingredients:

- 2 chicken breasts, grilled
- 4 slices bacon, cooked
- 2 slices cheddar cheese
- 4 sandwich rolls
- Lettuce
- Tomato slices
- Mayonnaise

Instructions:

1. Grill the chicken breasts and cook the bacon.
2. Toast the sandwich rolls and spread mayonnaise on each side.
3. Layer the sandwich with grilled chicken, bacon, cheddar cheese, lettuce, and tomato slices. Serve immediately.

Smoked Salmon and Cream Cheese Bagel

Ingredients:

- 2 bagels, split
- 4 ounces cream cheese
- 1/2 lb smoked salmon
- 1/4 red onion, thinly sliced
- Capers (optional)
- Fresh dill (optional)

Instructions:

1. Toast the bagels and spread cream cheese on both halves.
2. Layer the smoked salmon on the bagels and top with red onion slices, capers, and fresh dill.
3. Serve immediately.

Veggie and Hummus Wrap

Ingredients:

- 1 large tortilla wrap
- 1/2 cup hummus
- 1/2 cucumber, sliced
- 1/2 avocado, sliced
- 1/4 cup shredded carrots
- 1/4 cup spinach or lettuce
- 1/4 cup bell pepper, sliced

Instructions:

1. Spread hummus on the tortilla wrap.
2. Layer the cucumber, avocado, carrots, spinach, and bell pepper.
3. Roll up the wrap and serve immediately.

Grilled Chicken and Avocado Sandwich

Ingredients:

- 2 grilled chicken breasts
- 1 avocado, sliced
- 4 sandwich rolls
- Lettuce
- Tomato slices
- Mayonnaise

Instructions:

1. Grill the chicken breasts and slice the avocado.
2. Toast the sandwich rolls and spread mayonnaise on each side.
3. Layer the grilled chicken, avocado, lettuce, and tomato slices on the rolls. Serve immediately.

Croque Monsieur

Ingredients:

- 4 slices white bread
- 4 slices ham
- 4 slices Gruyère cheese
- 1/4 cup Dijon mustard
- 1/4 cup béchamel sauce (optional)

Instructions:

1. Spread Dijon mustard on one side of each slice of bread.
2. Layer ham and Gruyère cheese between the slices of bread.
3. Heat a skillet over medium heat and toast the sandwich on both sides until golden brown.
4. Optionally, pour béchamel sauce over the sandwich before serving.

BBQ Chicken Sliders

Ingredients:

- 2 chicken breasts, grilled and shredded
- 1/2 cup BBQ sauce
- 12 slider buns
- 1/2 cup coleslaw

Instructions:

1. Grill and shred the chicken breasts.
2. Toss the shredded chicken in BBQ sauce.
3. Toast the slider buns and fill with BBQ chicken and coleslaw. Serve immediately.

Chicken Caesar Wrap

Ingredients:

- 2 grilled chicken breasts, sliced
- 1 cup romaine lettuce, chopped
- 1/4 cup Caesar dressing
- 1/4 cup Parmesan cheese, shredded
- 1 large tortilla wrap

Instructions:

1. Toss the grilled chicken with romaine lettuce, Caesar dressing, and Parmesan cheese.
2. Place the mixture in the center of the tortilla wrap and roll it up tightly.
3. Serve immediately.

Reuben Sandwich

Ingredients:

- 4 slices rye bread
- 4 ounces corned beef, sliced
- 4 slices Swiss cheese
- 1/4 cup sauerkraut
- 2 tablespoons Russian dressing
- Butter for grilling

Instructions:

1. Spread Russian dressing on one side of each slice of rye bread.
2. Layer corned beef, Swiss cheese, and sauerkraut on the bread.
3. Grill the sandwich in a skillet with butter until golden brown on both sides. Serve immediately.

Chicken and Waffle Sandwich

Ingredients:

- 2 waffles (homemade or frozen)
- 2 fried chicken tenders
- 2 slices cheddar cheese
- Maple syrup

Instructions:

1. Cook the waffles and fry the chicken tenders.
2. Place a fried chicken tender and a slice of cheddar cheese between two waffles.
3. Drizzle with maple syrup and serve immediately.

Caprese Sandwich

Ingredients:

- 2 slices ciabatta bread
- 4 slices fresh mozzarella
- 2 tomatoes, sliced
- Fresh basil leaves
- Balsamic glaze
- Olive oil

Instructions:

1. Toast the ciabatta bread slices lightly.
2. Layer the mozzarella, tomatoes, and basil on one slice of bread.
3. Drizzle with balsamic glaze and olive oil.
4. Top with the other slice of bread and serve immediately.

Bacon, Egg, and Cheese Biscuit

Ingredients:

- 2 fresh biscuits (homemade or store-bought)
- 2 slices bacon
- 1 egg
- 2 slices cheddar cheese

Instructions:

1. Cook the bacon in a skillet until crispy.
2. Fry the egg to your preferred doneness.
3. Cut the biscuits in half and layer with the cooked bacon, egg, and cheddar cheese.
4. Serve immediately.

Tuna Salad Sandwich

Ingredients:

- 2 slices whole wheat bread
- 1 can tuna, drained
- 2 tablespoons mayonnaise
- 1 tablespoon Dijon mustard
- 1 tablespoon relish or chopped pickles
- Lettuce

Instructions:

1. Mix the tuna, mayonnaise, Dijon mustard, and relish in a bowl.
2. Spread the tuna salad on one slice of bread.
3. Top with lettuce and close the sandwich. Serve immediately.

BLT with Avocado

Ingredients:

- 2 slices toasted bread
- 4 slices bacon, cooked
- 2 slices tomato
- 1/2 avocado, sliced
- Lettuce
- Mayonnaise

Instructions:

1. Spread mayonnaise on the toasted bread slices.
2. Layer with bacon, tomato, avocado slices, and lettuce.
3. Close the sandwich and serve immediately.

Meatball Sub

Ingredients:

- 1 sub roll
- 4-6 meatballs (cooked)
- 1/2 cup marinara sauce
- 1/4 cup shredded mozzarella cheese
- Fresh basil (optional)

Instructions:

1. Heat the meatballs in marinara sauce.
2. Slice the sub roll and warm it in the oven or on a skillet.
3. Place the meatballs in the roll and top with marinara sauce and mozzarella cheese.
4. Place the sandwich under the broiler until the cheese is melted.
5. Garnish with fresh basil if desired, and serve.

Chicken and Pesto Panini

Ingredients:

- 2 slices sourdough or ciabatta bread
- 1 grilled chicken breast, sliced
- 2 tablespoons pesto sauce
- 1/4 cup mozzarella cheese, shredded
- Arugula or spinach

Instructions:

1. Spread pesto sauce on one slice of bread.
2. Layer the grilled chicken, mozzarella cheese, and arugula on the bread.
3. Close the sandwich and grill it in a panini press or skillet until crispy and golden brown.
4. Serve immediately.

Philly Chicken Cheesesteak

Ingredients:

- 1 hoagie roll
- 1 chicken breast, thinly sliced
- 1/2 onion, sliced
- 1/2 bell pepper, sliced
- 1/2 cup provolone cheese, shredded
- Olive oil for cooking

Instructions:

1. Heat olive oil in a skillet and sauté the onion and bell pepper until soft.
2. Add the sliced chicken to the pan and cook until browned.
3. Place the chicken, onions, and peppers on the hoagie roll.
4. Top with provolone cheese and melt under the broiler or in the skillet.
5. Serve immediately.

Egg Salad Sandwich with Pickles

Ingredients:

- 2 slices whole grain or white bread
- 2 hard-boiled eggs, chopped
- 2 tablespoons mayonnaise
- 1 tablespoon Dijon mustard
- 1 tablespoon pickles, chopped
- Lettuce

Instructions:

1. Mix the chopped eggs, mayonnaise, Dijon mustard, and pickles in a bowl.
2. Spread the egg salad on one slice of bread.
3. Top with lettuce and close the sandwich. Serve immediately.

Grilled Veggie and Mozzarella Sandwich

Ingredients:

- 2 slices whole wheat bread
- 1 zucchini, thinly sliced
- 1 eggplant, thinly sliced
- 1 red bell pepper, sliced
- 1/4 cup fresh mozzarella, sliced
- Olive oil for grilling
- Balsamic vinegar

Instructions:

1. Grill or roast the zucchini, eggplant, and bell pepper until tender.
2. Toast the bread slices and drizzle with balsamic vinegar.
3. Layer the grilled vegetables and mozzarella on the bread.
4. Close the sandwich and serve immediately.

Smoked Brisket Sandwich

Ingredients:

- 1 sandwich roll or brioche bun
- 1/2 lb smoked brisket, sliced
- 2 tablespoons BBQ sauce
- Pickled onions (optional)
- Fresh cilantro (optional)

Instructions:

1. Warm the smoked brisket in a skillet with BBQ sauce.
2. Slice the sandwich roll or bun and toast it lightly.
3. Layer the warm brisket on the roll and top with pickled onions and cilantro.
4. Serve immediately.

Fried Green Tomato BLT

Ingredients:

- 2 slices toasted sourdough bread
- 4 slices bacon, cooked
- 2 large green tomatoes, sliced
- 1/4 cup flour
- 1/4 cup cornmeal
- 1 egg, beaten
- Lettuce
- Mayonnaise

Instructions:

1. Coat the green tomato slices in flour, cornmeal, and dip them into the beaten egg.
2. Fry the tomatoes in hot oil until golden brown and crispy.
3. Spread mayonnaise on the toasted bread, then layer with bacon, fried green tomatoes, and lettuce.
4. Serve immediately.

Crab Cake Sandwich with Remoulade

Ingredients:

- 1 sandwich bun
- 1 large crab cake, cooked
- 2 tablespoons remoulade sauce
- Lettuce
- Tomato slices

Instructions:

1. Toast the sandwich bun and spread a generous amount of remoulade sauce on both sides.
2. Place the cooked crab cake on the bun.
3. Top with lettuce and tomato slices.
4. Close the sandwich and serve.

Grilled Cheese with Apple and Bacon

Ingredients:

- 2 slices of whole wheat or sourdough bread
- 2 slices cheddar cheese
- 4 slices bacon, cooked
- 1 small apple, thinly sliced
- Butter for grilling

Instructions:

1. Butter one side of each slice of bread.
2. Place a slice of cheddar cheese, bacon, and apple slices between the bread slices.
3. Grill the sandwich on medium heat until golden brown on both sides and the cheese is melted.
4. Serve immediately.

Mahi Mahi Fish Tacos

Ingredients:

- 2 small flour or corn tortillas
- 2 mahi mahi fillets, grilled or pan-seared
- Shredded cabbage
- Avocado slices
- Lime wedges
- Cilantro
- Salsa or crema

Instructions:

1. Grill or pan-sear the mahi mahi fillets until fully cooked.
2. Warm the tortillas and place the fish fillets on top.
3. Add shredded cabbage, avocado slices, and top with salsa or crema.
4. Garnish with cilantro and serve with lime wedges.

Grilled Tuna Melt

Ingredients:

- 2 slices sourdough bread
- 1 can tuna, drained
- 2 tablespoons mayonnaise
- 2 slices Swiss cheese
- 1 small onion, sliced
- Butter for grilling

Instructions:

1. Mix the tuna with mayonnaise and a pinch of salt.
2. Layer one slice of bread with the tuna mixture, cheese, and onion.
3. Top with the second slice of bread and butter the outside.
4. Grill the sandwich until golden brown and the cheese is melted.
5. Serve immediately.

Spicy Sausage and Peppers Sandwich

Ingredients:

- 1 hoagie roll
- 2 spicy sausages, cooked and sliced
- 1 red bell pepper, sliced
- 1 onion, sliced
- 1 tablespoon olive oil
- Hot sauce (optional)

Instructions:

1. Sauté the bell pepper and onion in olive oil until soft.
2. Warm the hoagie roll and fill it with the sliced sausage, sautéed peppers and onions.
3. Drizzle with hot sauce if desired.
4. Serve immediately.

Pulled BBQ Jackfruit Sandwich

Ingredients:

- 1 sandwich bun
- 1 can young green jackfruit, drained and shredded
- 1/2 cup BBQ sauce
- Pickled onions
- Coleslaw

Instructions:

1. Shred the jackfruit and cook it in a pan with BBQ sauce until tender.
2. Toast the sandwich bun and layer with the BBQ jackfruit, pickled onions, and coleslaw.
3. Serve immediately.

Italian Sub Sandwich

Ingredients:

- 1 hoagie roll
- 1/4 pound salami
- 1/4 pound pepperoni
- 1/4 pound ham
- 1/4 pound provolone cheese
- Lettuce, tomato, and onion
- Italian dressing or oil and vinegar

Instructions:

1. Slice the hoagie roll and layer with salami, pepperoni, ham, and provolone cheese.
2. Add lettuce, tomato, and onion, then drizzle with Italian dressing or oil and vinegar.
3. Close the sandwich and serve immediately.

Buffalo Chicken Wrap

Ingredients:

- 1 large flour tortilla
- 1 grilled chicken breast, sliced
- 2 tablespoons buffalo sauce
- Romaine lettuce
- 1/4 cup blue cheese crumbles
- 1 tablespoon ranch dressing

Instructions:

1. Toss the grilled chicken slices with buffalo sauce.
2. Lay the tortilla flat and add the buffalo chicken, lettuce, blue cheese, and ranch dressing.
3. Roll the tortilla up tightly and slice in half. Serve immediately.

Roast Beef and Swiss Sandwich

Ingredients:

- 2 slices rye or whole wheat bread
- 4-6 slices roast beef
- 2 slices Swiss cheese
- Dijon mustard or horseradish sauce
- Lettuce
- Tomato slices

Instructions:

1. Spread Dijon mustard or horseradish sauce on one side of the bread slices.
2. Layer roast beef and Swiss cheese on one slice of bread.
3. Add lettuce and tomato slices.
4. Top with the second slice of bread and serve immediately.

Breakfast Burrito Sandwich

Ingredients:

- 1 large flour tortilla
- 2 scrambled eggs
- 2 slices cooked bacon or sausage patties
- 1/4 cup shredded cheese
- Salsa or hot sauce
- Avocado slices
- Fresh cilantro

Instructions:

1. Scramble the eggs and cook the bacon or sausage.
2. Place the scrambled eggs, bacon or sausage, shredded cheese, and salsa on the tortilla.
3. Add avocado slices and cilantro for extra flavor.
4. Roll up the tortilla into a burrito and serve immediately.

Falafel Pita with Tzatziki

Ingredients:

- 1 pita bread
- 4-5 falafel balls, cooked
- 2 tablespoons tzatziki sauce
- Cucumber slices
- Tomato slices
- Fresh parsley

Instructions:

1. Warm the pita bread slightly and cut a pocket in the center.
2. Fill the pita with falafel balls, cucumber slices, tomato slices, and a dollop of tzatziki sauce.
3. Garnish with fresh parsley and serve immediately.

Philly Steak and Egg Sandwich

Ingredients:

- 1 hoagie roll
- 4-5 slices thinly sliced beef (ribeye or flank steak)
- 2 scrambled eggs
- 1/4 cup sautéed onions and bell peppers
- Provolone cheese slices
- Olive oil

Instructions:

1. Sauté the onions and bell peppers in olive oil until softened.
2. Cook the thinly sliced beef in the same pan until browned and cooked through.
3. Scramble the eggs in another pan.
4. Warm the hoagie roll and layer the beef, scrambled eggs, sautéed onions and peppers, and provolone cheese on the roll.
5. Serve immediately.

Cuban Sandwich

Ingredients:

- 1 Cuban-style bread or baguette
- 4-5 slices roasted pork
- 2 slices ham
- 2 slices Swiss cheese
- Pickles
- Yellow mustard
- Butter

Instructions:

1. Preheat a panini press or grill pan.
2. Slice the Cuban bread and spread mustard on one side.
3. Layer the roasted pork, ham, Swiss cheese, and pickles inside the bread.
4. Butter the outside of the bread and grill until crispy and golden, pressing it lightly as it cooks.
5. Serve immediately.

Veggie and Quinoa Wrap

Ingredients:

- 1 large whole wheat or spinach wrap
- 1/2 cup cooked quinoa
- 1/4 cup hummus
- Sliced cucumber
- Sliced bell peppers
- Fresh spinach or lettuce
- Grated carrots
- Feta cheese (optional)

Instructions:

1. Lay the wrap flat and spread hummus over the entire surface.
2. Add the quinoa, cucumber, bell peppers, spinach, and grated carrots on top.
3. Sprinkle with feta cheese if desired.
4. Roll up the wrap tightly, folding in the sides, and slice in half to serve.

Grilled Shrimp and Avocado Sandwich

Ingredients:

- 2 slices of toasted sandwich bread (whole wheat or sourdough)
- 6-8 grilled shrimp, peeled and deveined
- 1/2 avocado, sliced
- Romaine lettuce
- Tomato slices
- Mayonnaise or aioli
- Lime wedges

Instructions:

1. Grill shrimp until cooked through, and set aside.
2. Toast the bread slices and spread mayonnaise or aioli on each side.
3. Layer lettuce, tomato, grilled shrimp, and avocado slices on one slice of bread.
4. Squeeze fresh lime juice over the ingredients.
5. Top with the second slice of bread and serve immediately.

Lobster and Bacon Club Sandwich

Ingredients:

- 3 slices toasted white or whole wheat bread
- 1/2 cup cooked lobster meat
- 2 slices crispy bacon
- Romaine lettuce
- Tomato slices
- Mayonnaise or lemon aioli

Instructions:

1. Toast the bread and spread mayonnaise or lemon aioli on each slice.
2. Layer the lobster meat, bacon, lettuce, and tomato between the slices of bread.
3. Assemble the sandwich in a club-style, with three layers of bread.
4. Cut into quarters and serve immediately.

Spicy Chicken Banh Mi

Ingredients:

- 1 baguette
- 1 grilled chicken breast, thinly sliced
- 1/4 cup pickled carrots and daikon radish
- Sliced cucumber
- Fresh cilantro
- Jalapeño slices
- Mayonnaise or spicy sriracha mayo
- Soy sauce or fish sauce (optional)

Instructions:

1. Slice the baguette and spread mayonnaise or spicy sriracha mayo on both sides.
2. Layer the grilled chicken, pickled carrots and radish, cucumber, cilantro, and jalapeño slices.
3. Drizzle with a little soy sauce or fish sauce if desired.
4. Close the sandwich and serve immediately.

Grilled Salmon and Cucumber Sandwich

Ingredients:

- 2 slices whole-grain or multigrain bread
- 1 grilled salmon fillet
- Sliced cucumber
- Fresh dill
- Cream cheese or herbed butter
- Arugula or lettuce

Instructions:

1. Grill the salmon fillet and set aside to cool slightly.
2. Toast the bread and spread cream cheese or herbed butter on each slice.
3. Layer the grilled salmon, cucumber slices, fresh dill, and arugula on one slice of bread.
4. Top with the second slice of bread and serve immediately.

Pulled Chicken and Mango Slaw Sandwich

Ingredients:

- 1 sandwich roll or slider bun
- 1/2 cup pulled chicken (cooked and shredded)
- 1/4 cup mango slaw (shredded cabbage, mango, cilantro, lime, and a splash of vinegar)
- Jalapeño slices (optional)
- Fresh cilantro

Instructions:

1. Toast the sandwich roll or slider bun.
2. Add a generous amount of pulled chicken on the bottom bun.
3. Top with the mango slaw, jalapeño slices, and fresh cilantro.
4. Top with the other bun and serve immediately.

www.ingramcontent.com/pod-product-compliance
Lightning Source LLC
LaVergne TN
LVHW081501060526
838201LV00056BA/2863